I WILL LOOK FOR YOU AMONG THE STARS

by Kamala Kennedy

CHAPTERS

chapter one

grief

i remember the moment
i fell under your spell
and even the most dreary of
days
felt like summer

-under your spell

you peeled away
the protective layers
i had built around my soul

you uncovered me
in ways no one else
had ever done
before

-broken walls

take me
to your castle
in the clouds

show me
true beauty

-*true beauty*

i have been broken
twisted
lied to
poisoned
by their words

this is all
that is left
of me

-left of me

to be lonely
is to feel the hurt
of not being cared for
by others

-lonely

lock me in this fantasy
forever

i never want to leave

-if only i still had you

the piano keys play
almost by themselves
singing a sad melody
about you

-remembrance

death has taken
so many people from me
i wish i could travel back in
time
to when i was young
and be with them all
again

-*young*

i wish we could run away
to our own little world
together

-moonrise kingdom

my soul is speckled with loss
sprinkled with pain
weighed down with chains
and yet i am here
the phoenix
rising from the ashes

-the phoenix

the hardest part of love
is giving someone else
control
over how you feel

-*love is the art of giving up
control*

he may have left you
and it feels
as if he ripped out
a piece of your heart
as he left

but fear not
you will heal
and come back stronger
and more beautiful
than before

-*stronger*

there is something beautiful
in the echo of a cry
for pain comes out
and turns to music

-oblique

taste the beauty
of a summer breeze
breathe in gently
and let your soul relax

-believe

skinny dip with me
in the shallows of the cove
in the dead of night
let's make love on the beach
until the morning light

-love me

i find myself often wanting
things
i could never have
and first among them
is you

-you

you sweetened my tea with
sugar
you sweetened my life with
affection

-sweet

i could've shown you
so much beauty in this world
i could've given you
so much love

but you
didn't care

-eyes closed

plant flowers on my grave
when i die

even in death
i want to make the world
more beautiful

-grave

your picture
will always be
on my bedside table

every day i pray
that i never forget
your face

-*memories in stone*

never go back
to those
who hurt you

if they apologize
its because
they miss what you did
for them
they don't miss
who you are

-miss you

you turned my pain
to roses
you turned my darkness
to light

-sun

don't ever let them label you

-resist

take the power
over your own fate
into your own hands

-power

your love
made me feel
as if i had never
been loved
before

-something new

the end falls near
a perfect night
i don't want to say
goodbye

-*goodbye*

chapter two

darkness

no one ever tells you
how much it hurts
when you fall
this far

-fall this far

the darkness bites at my soul
like the cold of winter
i curl up
hoping to just
survive

-survive

there is nothing more
beautiful
in the human experience
than to have loved
and lost

-to have loved & lost

please, please
just stay the night
with me
i can't make it through
the darkness
alone

-alone

i miss your love
even if it came with
betrayal

-missing you

it breaks my heart
to say goodbye
to you

it's the hardest thing
i've ever had to do
but its also the most
necessary
thing

-*necessary*

my tears
dripping down my face
as you tell me
it's over

-*drip, drip*

you were my guiding wind
that steered my ship
through troubled waters

without you
i feel so lost

nowhere to go
no reason
to go on

-that place

i thought
i had glued myself
back together
until i saw you
with her
and i broke
all over again

-*all over again*

the worst part
about being in love
with a figment
of your own
imagination
is that no one
could ever live up
to the fantasy

-*"him"*

my thoughts lay strong
with feelings for you
as far as i fall
i can never escape
how much of me
is yours

-heartstrings

will you give her
what you never gave
me?

will you do all
the little things
like you never did
for me?

i agonize
over why
i seemingly
was never
worth it

-*worth it*

everything is okay

-the greatest lie

i have never been
so enshrouded in darkness
as i am
trying
to get over
you

-god help me

everything is wrong
without you

-simple, painful, truthful

kiss me
let me imagine
you're him
so i can have
one last taste
of paradise

-paradise

i wish i could smile
without
pretending

-faux

i wish i had never tasted
true happiness

if i had remained ignorant
i couldn't crave
what i didn't know

having tasted true happiness
is the greatest of blessings
and the cruelest of curses

-cruelest of curses

i curse you
under my breath
for trespassing
on my mind

-mind

the tragedy
of being hurt
is watching yourself become
-in some small way-
what hurt you

-*hurt me*

i know we have to say
goodbye

i wish i could stretch
this moment
out into a million years

it hurts too much

-*slow goodbye*

i don't care
if its a lie
just tell me
you miss me

-*sweet nothings*

i know this isn't love
and obsession isn't healthy
but that
won't stop me

-*shine*

we disappear
just more shadows
in the darkness

-disappear

everything
is dark
in the place
where we
are separated

-tragedy, me oh my

chapter two

loss

you haunt me

even in my good dreams
there is a tinge
of missing you
and it kills me

-dreams

why wasn't i
good enough
for you?

-closure

you never cared
about me
and i hate myself
because
i can't stop
caring
about you
in return

-*alternate endings*

talk to me
please
give me a hand
and guide me out
of this cloud
of darkness

-guide

i miss
everything

about
us

-*v*

i just cant get you
off my mind

-*sickness*

i've been through
many things
in my life

but nothing hurt
as much
as loving
you

-loving you

i want to warn
everyone who comes
after me

about how much it hurts
to be loved by you
but how hard it is
to stop

-arrete

#resist
#resist
#resist

-resist the dictator

the curve
of your smile
never leaves
my mind

-curve

take me
to all
the romantic places

seduce me
in beautiful ways

i want to give you
everything

-melody

perhaps it would be better for
me
to gouge out my eyes
so that i couldn't see you

at least then
i could protect
my fragile heart
from thoughts
of you

-heart ache

please, don't watch me cry
i don't want you to see me
like this

-broken

why am i addicted
to loving
the person
who broke me?

-cruel heart

watch carefully
how others
treat you

if they turn their backs
in your darkest hour
they were never
truly
good to you

-ivx

you asked
for a second chance
for the millionth time

and like a broken fool
i couldn't say no

-addiction

i know i can't drown
your memory
with alcohol
but i'm going to try

-*what else can i do?*

us lonely souls
must stick together

we are the only ones
who understand

-community of pain

art
is the respite
of the broken

-respite

only lonely people
like you and me
end up
in places like this

-lonely people

i wish
i could
drink
your memory
away

-*solace*

broken people
break people

-*vicious cycle*

i listen to our song
and remember
the good times
we had

-recycling pain

losing you
was the worst thing
that ever happened
to my fragile heart

-glass

chapter four

hope

i woke up this morning
feeling, for the first time
in a long time
somewhat close
to normal

-beginning of recovery

the clouds
begin
to part

the sun
begins
to shine

-*shine*

like a broken bone
a broken heart
heals
stronger
than it was before

-*heal*

we can change things
if only
we have
the audacity
to believe
we can

-audacity

sometimes
we just have to trust
that things
will eventually work out

*-what else do we have but
hope?*

even if i die
destitute and poor
at least
my memories of you
will be forever mine

-remember

ignorance
is a disease

-*society*

there is nothing like
the strength
of a woman
rebuilding herself
after being broken

-strength xx

recovery
always feels impossible

but don't worry
you will get
through this

-don't worry

if there is an afterlife
i hope
it's one
where i get to relive
our best moments
over and over again

-heaven

resenting those
who hurt you
is murder-suicide

-crime

strength
is not the view
from the highest mountain

strength
is the process
of climbing

-climb

ignore my past
let's build
a future

-build

break the pattern
leave what hurt you
be free

-*while you have the strength
to leave, do it*

the future is female
and all the better
for it

-female

never bet against
a woman
who has her back
against the wall

she will rise
she will defeat all odds
she will win

-*victory*

with a devious look
you invited me
into a world of trouble
i fell in with you
with gleeful abandon

-gleeful abandon

i gave you the best of me
and that wasn't enough
i guess i have to come
to terms
with that

-pain

i know i will never
see you again
and so
i will look for you
among the stars
hoping
that these constellations
will guide me
back to you

-*stars*

fear
is the death
of success

-fear nothing

i want to see a future
with women in government
and people
of all identities
coexisting
together

-beautiful dream

i saw you sleeping there
looking so beautiful
laying on that pillow

-my most cherished memory

i am glad
that i felt
the worst of heartbreak

now i know
how to love someone
all the more beautifully

-beautiful

all shapes
all sizes
all identities
all people

-all beautiful

i hope this book
gave you hope
gave you healing
gave you solace
in this darkness
we call life

i hope
i gave you
something good

*-this is my love letter to every
broken soul in the world*

Made in the USA
Las Vegas, NV
25 August 2022

54039779R00066